VIV RICHARDS COLOR

WEST INDIES CRICKETER

MR VIVEK KUMAR PANDEY

Made with ♥ on the Notion Press Platform
www.notionpress.com

Contents

Foreword

Short Biography Of Viv Richards & Life Style, Career etc. During Writing This Book No Character, No Religion & No Caste Are Harmed. It's Only For Study Purpose. We don't want to hurt anyone. This Book Fully Color Editions

Preface

Author biography in English :

MY NAME IS VIVEK KUMAR PANDEY . I WAS BORN IN 30 SEP 2002,I AM FROM SURAT GUJARAT INDIA.MY DREAM WAS TO BE GOOD WRITERS ,MY FAMILY SUPPORTED ME TO SUCCESSFUL AND I CAN DO IT MY SELF.How do I write? That is a question, I believe, that can be honestly answered by me."CELEBRATING YOUNGEST WRITER AWARD WINNER IN GUJARAT 1ST RANK" MR PANDEY JI . I may think I did a good job writing something. The reader is the one who decides the quality of my writing. I do find writing to be natural to me and therefore find it to be a real challenge. My trick as a challenged writer is to do the best I can and know that I am happy with the final outcome. It may take a while to do my best and there may be quite a few problems I run into along the way.

I am not a greedy person those who are thinking about me and my self I never tried it anyone people suffering from sadness ,I trying to get promoted people suffering from happiness and joy in your Life Time. Now in current situation in India and also world people are unemployed and have no many but our indian governor help to people to get free food from ration card , i also take part in leadership team ,i am Motivational speaker , Film script writer. There was my two dream firstly writer and secondly actor & also my own film is upcoming soon i done almost completely completed script for my film .I AM GOING TO SAY WORD OF HEART TOUCH OUT PLEASE READ IT" , firstly i thanks my father he supports me in this field they always getting inspired me by own his words and behavior ,they always said that he was a biggest person in the world in future and also they purchase fruit and chocolate for me in anytime & anyway , firstly my father buy him then call me Vivek you want a chocolate i will say yes papa but how many tell me ,papa: you tell me how much i buy him i told 1 or 2 chocolate but my father purchase whole the boxes of chocolate and they get suprised me. MY FATHER WAS BORN IN " 20 SEPTEMBER" 1971 IN INDIA.

1) MY FATHER FAVORITE CLOTHES IS KURTA PAIJMA AND ALSO STYLES SHOE

2) FAVORITE SINGER IS KISHORE DA

3) FAVORITE STATE GUJARAT AND KOLKATA , HIS VILLAGE IN BIHAR

4) FAVORITE COLOR BLACK AND WHITE

THEY ALSO LOVE cricket like IPL and one day t-20 .they also like watching a News daily and heard the song daily ,they also interested in tik tok video but in current time tik tok is banned in india but also few videos are in you tube. In lockdown time my family and me very enjoy day daily. my father play daily ludo with his sister and son, daughter.they always loved tea and coffee anytime call me . I make it tea for my father but some reason after the April to june they are suffering from fever and cough , weakness on 6 June 2020 my father death. they not told me say bye bye his life. After death of 6 June on 10 june my mom and dad anniversary.but my father is Best in the world they can do anything for me please take care of father and respect it of your parents.

ONE
VIV RICHARDS

- **Viv Richards Color**

1. Short Biography Of Viv Richards & Life Style, Career etc. During Writing This Book No Character, No Religion & No Caste Are Harmed. It's Only For Study Purpose. We don't want to hurt anyone.

Viv Richards (born 7 March 1952) is an Antiguan retired cricketer who represented the West Indies cricket team between 1974 and 1991. Batting generally at number three in a dominant West Indies side, Richards is widely regarded as one of the greatest batsmen of all time.

Richards made his test debut in 1974 against India along with Gordon Greenidge. His best years were between 1976 and 1983 where he averaged a remarkable 66.51 with the bat in test cricket. In 1984 he suffered from pterygium and had an eye surgery which affected his eyesight and reflexes. Despite this, he remained the best batsman in the world for the next four years, averaging 50. His form declined in the latter years of his career where he averaged 36. Overall,

Richards scored 8,540 runs in 121 Test matches at an average of 50.23, including 24 centuries. He also scored 1281 runs in World Series Cricket with five tons at average of over 55 which was regarded as highest and most difficult cricket ever played. As a captain, he won 27 of 50 Test matches and lost only 8. He also scored nearly 7,000 runs in One Day Internationals and more than 36,000 in first-class cricket.

He was knighted for his contributions to cricket in 1999. In 2000 he was voted one of Wisden's five Cricketers of the Century by a 100-member panel of experts and in 2002 the almanack judged that he had played the best One Day International innings of all time. In December 2002, he was chosen by Wisden as the greatest One Day International batsman who had played to that date and as the third greatest Test cricket batter. In 2009, Richards was inducted into the ICC Cricket Hall of Fame.

In October 2013, Wisden selected the best test team across 150 years of test history and slotted Viv at number 3 slot, he was only batsman of post war era along with Sachin Tendulkar to get featured in that team.

· **Viv Richards life**

Richards was born to Malcolm and Gretel Richards in St. John's, Antigua, then part of the British Leeward Islands. He attended St. John's Boys Primary School and then Antigua Grammar Secondary School on a scholarship. Richards discovered cricket at a young age. His brothers, Mervyn and Donald, both played the game, representing Antigua as amateurs, and they encouraged him to play. The young Viv initially practised with his father and Pat Evanson, a neighbour and family friend, who had captained the

Antigua side.

Richards left school aged 18, and worked at D'Arcy's Bar and Restaurant in St. John's. He joined St. John's Cricket Club and the owner of the restaurant where he worked, D'Arcy Williams, provided him with new whites, gloves, pads and a bat. After a few seasons with St. John's C.C., he joined Rising Sun Cricket Club, where he remained until his departure to play abroad.

· Viv Richards Cricket career

Richards made his first-class debut in January 1972 when he was 19. He took part in a non-competition match, representing the Leeward Islands against the Windwards: Richards made 20 and 26. His competitive debut followed a few days later. Playing in the domestic West Indian Shell Shield for the Combined Leeward and Windward Islands in Kingston, Jamaica versus Jamaica, he scored 15 and 32, top-scoring in the second innings in a heavy defeat for his side.

By the time Richards was 22, he had played matches in the Antigua, Leeward Islands and Combined Islands tournaments. In 1973, his abilities were noticed by Len Creed, Vice Chairman at Somerset, who was in Antigua at the time as part of a West Country touring side. Surrey had earlier rejected both Richards and Andy Roberts at the Surrey Indoor Nets in late 1972. "They did not think we were good enough even to further our cricket education."

· Viv Richards Move to England, 1973–1974

Richards relocated to the United Kingdom, where Creed arranged for him to play league cricket for Lansdown C.C. in Bath. He made his Lansdown debut, as part of the second

XI, at Weston-super-Mare on 26 April 1973. Richards was also employed by the club as assistant groundsman to head groundsman, John Heyward, to allow him some financial independence until his career was established. After his debut he was promoted to the first team where he was introduced to the Lansdown all-rounder "Shandy" Perera from Ceylon (now Sri Lanka). Richards cites Perera as a major influence on his cricket development especially with regards to post-game analysis. He finished his first season at Lansdown top of the batting averages and shortly afterwards was offered a two-year contract with county side Somerset.

Richards then moved to Taunton in 1974 in preparation for his professional debut with Somerset CCC where he was assigned living accommodation by the club; a flat-share with two other county players: Ian Botham and Dennis Breakwell. On 27 April 1974 Richards made his Benson & Hedges Cup debut for Somerset against Glamorgan in Swansea; after the game Somerset skipper Brian Close arranged a player's ovation for Richards in recognition of his playing and contribution to the victory. Richards was awarded Man of the Match.

- **Viv Richards Test debut to international stardom, 1975–1984**

Richards made his Test match debut for the West Indian cricket team in 1974 against India in Bangalore. He made an unbeaten 192 in the second Test of the same series in New Delhi. The West Indies saw him as a strong opener and he kept his profile up in the early years of his promising career.

In 1975 Richards helped the West Indies to win the inaugural Cricket World Cup final, a feat he later described as the most memorable of his career. He starred in the field, running out Alan Turner, Ian Chappell and Greg Chappell. The West Indies were again able to win the following World Cup in 1979, thanks to a Richards century in the final at Lord's, and Richards believes that on both occasions, despite internal island divisions, the Caribbean came together.

He was until 2005 the only man to score a century and take 5 wickets in the same one-day international, against New Zealand at Dunedin in 1986–87. He rescued his side from a perilous position at Old Trafford in 1984 and, in partnership with Michael Holding, smashed 189 to win the game off his own bat.

1976 was perhaps Richards' finest year: he scored 1710 runs, at an astonishing average of 90.00, with seven centuries in 11 Tests. This achievement is all the more remarkable considering he missed the second Test at Lord's after contracting glandular fever; yet he returned to score his career-best 291 at the Oval later in the summer. This tally stood as the world record for most Test runs by a batsman in a single calendar year for 30 years until broken by Mohammad Yousuf of Pakistan on 30 November 2006.

Richards had a long and successful career in the County Championship in England, playing for many years for Somerset. In 1983, the team won the NatWest Trophy, with Richards and close friend Ian Botham having a playful slugging match in the final few overs. Richards also starred in Somerset's victores in the finals of the 1979 Gillette Cup, and the 1981 Benson & Hedges Cup, making a century in both finals, also helping Somerset to win the 1979 John Player League and the 1982 Benson & Hedges Cup.Richards refused a "blank-cheque" offer to play for a rebel West Indies squad in South Africa during the Apartheid era in

1983, and again in 1984.

· **Viv Richards West Indies captain**

Richards captained the West Indies in 50 Test matches from 1984 to 1991. He is the only West Indies captain never to lose a Test series, and it is said that his fierce will to win contributed to this achievement. His captaincy was, however, not without controversy: one incident was his aggressive, "finger-flapping" appeal leading to the incorrect dismissal of England batsman Rob Bailey in the Barbados Test in 1990, which was described by Wisden as "at best undignified and unsightly. At worst, it was calculated gamesmanship". This behaviour would nowadays be penalised according to Section 2.5. of the Rules of Conduct of the ICC Code of Conduct.

During a match against Zimbabwe during the 1983 Cricket World Cup, Richards returned to the crease after a stoppage for bad light and accidentally took strike at the wrong end, which remains a very rare occurrence.

Richards made his highest first-class score, 322, for Somerset again Warwickshire in 1985. However, despite his totemic presence at Somerset, over time his performances declined as he devoted most of his time to international cricket. The county finished bottom of the County Championship in 1985, and next to bottom in 1986. New team captain Peter Roebuck became the centre of a major controversy when he was instrumental in the county's decision not to renew the contracts of Richards and his West Indies teammate Joel Garner for the 1987 season, whose runs and wickets had brought the county much success in the previous eight years.

Somerset proposed to replace the pair with New Zealand batsman Martin Crowe. Consequently, Ian Botham refused a new contract with Somerset in protest at the way his friends Richards and Garner had been treated and promptly joined Worcestershire. After many years of bitterness over the event and the eventual removal of Roebuck from the club, Richards was eventually honoured with the naming of a set of entrance gates after him at the County Ground, Taunton.

After his sacking from Somerset, Richards spent the 1987 season in the Lancashire League playing as Rishton CC's professional, in preparation for the West Indies tour the following season.In November 1988, while on tour of Australia with the West Indies, Richards became the first West Indies player to reach 100 first-class centuries by scoring 101 against New South Wales. Richards remains the only West Indies player to achieve this milestone, and among non-England qualified players only Don Bradman (117) scored more first-class centuries than Richards' 114.Richards returned to county cricket for the 1990 season towards the end of his career to play for Glamorgan, helping them to win the AXA Sunday League in 1993.

- **Viv Richards being interviewed after a cricket match in 2006**

Richards is a commentator on BBC's Test Match Special (TMS). He participated in Prince Edward of the United Kingdom's 1987 charity television special The Grand Knockout Tournament. He was featured in the 2010 documentary movie Fire in Babylon and spoke about his experiences playing for the West Indies. Richards joined the Delhi Daredevils as their mentor in The Indian Premier

League in 2013, and also mentored the Quetta Gladiators in the 2016, 2017, 2018, 2019, 2020 and 2022 Pakistan Super League.

· **Viv Richards Personality and playing style**

Quiet and self-contained away from the pitch, Richards was a very powerful right-handed batsman with an extremely attacking style, "possibly the most destructive batsman the sport has ever seen". He was also an excellent fielder and a more than competent off-spin bowler. He is often regarded as the most physically devastating and exciting batsman that ever played the game by cricketers, journalists, fans and others alike, and played his entire 17-year career without a helmet.

His fearless and aggressive style of play, and relaxed but determined demeanor made him a great crowd favourite and an intimidating prospect for opposition bowlers all over the world. The word "swagger" is frequently used to describe his batting style. His batting often completely dominated opposing bowlers. He had the ability to drive good-length balls from outside off-stump through midwicket, his trademark shot, and was one of the great exponents of the hook shot.

Viv Richards was notorious for punishing bowlers that dared to sledge him, so much so, that many opposing captains banned their players from the practice. However playing for Somerset in a county game against Glamorgan, Greg Thomas attempted to sledge Richards after he had played and missed at several balls in a row. He sarcastically informed Richards: "It's red, round and it's about five ounces, in case you were wondering." Richards then hammered the next delivery for 6, straight out of the stadium and into a nearby river. Turning back to the bowler, he commented: "You know what it looks like, now go and find it."

- **Viv Richards Hitting Across the Line**

In 1991, Richards published his autobiography entitled Hitting Across the Line. In the book, Richards describes how his whole life revolved around sports, cricket in particular. Of special interest is his technique, expressed by the title of the book. To hit across the line of the ball is considered taboo, and dangerously risky. However, Richards' explanation of the conditions in which he played cricket in Antigua as a child, explains how this technique came to be.

- **Viv Richards' Test career batting chart**

In his Test career, he scored 8,540 runs in 121 Test matches at an average of 50.23. Richards also scored 5 centuries in World Series Cricket between 1977 and 1979. These are not recognised by the ICC as "official" Test centuries. Richards won 27 of 50 matches as a Test captain, and lost only 8. He is also the scorer of the equal second fastest-ever Test century, from just 56 balls against England in Antigua during the 1986 tour. He hit 84 sixes in Test cricket. His highest innings of 291 is equal seventh on the list of West Indies' highest individual scores.

- **Viv Richards International records**

1. In 1986, Richards became the first batsman to score a Test century at a strike rate of over 150.

2. Richards scored the fastest century in Test history (56 balls) in 1986, being sole record holder until his feat was first equalled by Misbah-ul-Haq in 2014 and then eclipsed by Brendon McCullum's 54-ball ton in 2016.

3. Richards set a record for being the fastest batsman to 1,000 ODI runs (21 innings); this record has subsequently been equalled by Kevin Pietersen, Babar Azam, Jonathan Trott and Quinton de Kock.

4. Along with Michael Holding, Richards holds the record for the highest ever 10th wicket partnership in ODI history.(106*)

5. He also holds the record for the highest individual ODI score when batting at number 4 position (189*)

6. He became the first player to score a fifty and to take a five wicket haul in the same ODI. He also became the first cricketer to score a century as well as to take a five wicket haul in the same ODI match.

7. Richards was the first player to complete the double of scoring 1000 runs and taking 50 wickets in ODI history.

• **The Sir Vivian Richards Stadium in 2012**

In 1994, Richards was appointed an Officer of the Order of the British Empire (OBE) for services to cricket. In 1999, he was made a Knight Commander of the Order of the Nation (KCN) by his native country Antigua and Barbuda. In 2006, he was upgraded to Antigua and Barbuda highest award, Knight of the Order of the National Hero (KNH).

The Sir Vivian Richards Stadium in North Sound, Antigua, is named in his honour. It was built for use in the 2007 Cricket World Cup. The ground has hosted three Test matches, as well as a number of One-Day Internationals and T20 Internationals.The Richards–Botham Trophy, replacing the Wisden Trophy for winners of West Indies–England Test series, is named in honour of Richards and Sir Ian Botham.In 2022, Richards was awarded the Order of the Caribbean Community (OOC), the highest honour that can be conferred upon a Caribbean national. The award confers the styling "The Honourable" as well.

In 2000, Richards was named one of the five Wisden Cricketers of the Century, coming fifth behind Sir Donald Bradman, Sir Garfield Sobers, Sir Jack Hobbs and Shane Warne in the poll of 100 international cricket experts appointed by Wisden Cricketers' Almanack.

Several prominent personalities including former cricketer Imran Khan and writer John Birmingham are of the opinion that Richards was the best ever batsman against genuine fast bowling. For Barry Richards, Ravi Shastri and Neil Fairbrother, he has been cited as the best batsman they personally witnessed. Wasim Akram rates Richards the greatest batsman he ever bowled to, ahead of Sunil Gavaskar and Martin Crowe.

Akram also rates Richards as the best and most complete batsman he ever saw ahead of Sachin Tendulkar and Brian Lara. Crowe himself rated Richards as the best batsman he played against, along with Greg Chappell. Arguably the two greatest spinners ever, Muthiah Muralitharan and Shane Warne both idolize Richards. Murali idolized Richards in his years growing up, while Warne rates him the greatest batsman "for me", and overall just after Bradman.

If you talk about a batsman with an unmatched technique, charisma and someone who had a huge impact on the game, it is Sir Vivian Richards. I have played against all the greats from mid-eighties to the nineties to the 2000s, but Viv Richards was a class apart.

· **Wasim Akram on Viv Richards**

Ian Botham who is regarded as one of the greatest all-rounders of all time and one of England's greatest cricketers, rates Richards as the greatest batsman he ever saw ahead of Sunil Gavaskar, Greg Chappell, Martin Crowe, Sachin Tendulkar and Brian Lara. Michael Holding, often regarded as one of the greatest fast bowlers of all time and part of the West Indies four-prolonged pace attack during the late 1970s and early 1980s rates Richards as the greatest batsman he witnessed in the last 50 years. England's fast bowling great Bob Willis rated Viv as greatest batsman he ever witnessed and best he ever bowled to.At number 3:- Viv Richards; I never saw Donald Bradman play but if he was better player then Viv then he must have been some player.

Australian fast bowling greats Jeff Thomson often regarded as the fastest bowler in cricket history along with Dennis Lillee rates Richards as best batsman they ever bowled against. Lillee rates Richards as best batsman he bowled to and went on to say him as The Supreme player. Thomson also rates Richards as the greatest batsman he bowled against. Former Australian captain Ian Chappell who is regarded as one of the best cricket captains of all time rates Richards as the most intimidating and dangerous batsman he ever saw who often changed games simply by walking to the crease.For sheer ability to rip an attack apart with animal like brutality and still maintaining better consistency then all others around. I have to pick Viv on top of the list. I just love bowling to the man because it was such a challenge. I regard him as the supreme player. I think we finished about level- I got him as often as he got me

Brian Lara and Sachin Tendulkar who are regarded as two of the greatest modern day batsman rates Richards as the best they ever saw and their batting idol while growing up. Kumar Sangakara, former Sri Lankan Wicket keeper batsman often rates Richards along with Lara as the greatest batsman he ever witnessed and further calls Richards as his cricketing idol while growing up. Former Pakistan captain Inzamam-ul-haq rates Richards as the greatest batsman he ever saw ahead of both Tendulkar and Lara.

The ICC has produced rankings for batsmen and bowlers for both the longer and shorter versions. In the ratings for Test Cricket, Richards holds the equal seventh highest peak rating (938), after Sir Donald Bradman (961), Steve Smith (947), Sir Len Hutton, Sir Jack Hobbs, Ricky Ponting and Peter May. The ODI ratings placed Richards in first followed by Zaheer Abbas and Greg Chappell. He topped the rankings at the end of the years 1976, 1977, 1980, 1981, 1982, 1983 and 1986.

He was voted the greatest cricketer since 1970 in a poll, ahead of Ian Botham and Shane Warne. That poll saw both Botham and Warne vote for Richards, and in the opinions of both, Richards is the greatest batsman they ever saw. In 2006, in a study done by a team of ESPN's Cricinfo magazine, Richards was again chosen as the greatest ODI Batsman ever.To mark 150 years of the Cricketers' Almanack, Wisden named him in an all-time Test World XI.

Some writers contend that Richards also played international football for Antigua and Barbuda, appearing in qualifying matches for the 1974 World Cup. However, he does not appear in recorded line-ups for these matches.

· **Viv Richards Personal life**

Richards and his wife Miriam have two children, including Mali, who has also played first-class cricket. Richards is also godfather to Ian Botham's son, Liam.Richards had a brief relationship with Indian actress Neena Gupta, with whom he has a daughter, fashion designer Masaba Gupta.

TWO

HISTORY OF THE WEST INDIES CRICKET TEAM

- **History of the West Indies cricket team**

The history of the West Indian cricket team begins in the 1880s when the first combined West Indian team was formed and toured Canada and the United States. In the 1890s, the first representative sides were selected to play visiting English sides. Administered by the West Indies Cricket Board ("WICB"), and known colloquially as The Windies, the West Indies cricket team represents a sporting confederation of English-speaking Caribbean countries.

The WICB joined the sport's international ruling body, the Imperial Cricket Conference, in 1926, and played their first official international match, which in cricket is called a Test, in 1928.Although blessed with some great players in their early days as a Test nation, their successes remained sporadic until the 1960s, by which time the side had changed from a white-dominated to a black-dominated side. By the late 1970s, the West Indies had a side recognised as unofficial world champions, a title they retained throughout the 1980s.

Their team from the 1970s and 1980s is now widely regarded as having been one of the best in test cricket's history, alongside Don Bradman's Invincibles. During these glory years, the Windies were noted for their four-man fast bowling attack, backed up by some of the best batsmen in the world. The 1980s saw them set a then-record streak of 11 consecutive Test victories in 1984, which was part of a still-standing record of 27 tests without defeat , as well as inflicting two 5–0 "blackwashes" against the old enemy of England. Throughout the 1990s and 2000s, however, West Indian cricket declined, in part due to the rise in popularity of athletics and football in West Indian countries, and the team today is struggling to regain its past glory.

In their early days in the 1930s, the side represented the British colonies of the West Indies Federation plus British Guyana. The current side represents the now independent states of Antigua and Barbuda, Barbados, Dominica, Grenada, Guyana, Jamaica, Saint Kitts and Nevis, Saint Lucia, Saint Vincent and the Grenadines and Trinidad and Tobago, and the British dependencies of Anguilla, Montserrat and the British Virgin Islands along with the U.S. Virgin Islands and St. Maarten.National teams also exist for the various islands, which, as they are all separate countries, very much keep their local identities and support their local favourites. These national teams take part in the West Indian first-class competition, the Stanford 20/20, the Carib Beer Cup . It is also common for other international teams to play the island teams for warm-up games before they take on the combined West Indies team.

- **tours**

The first major international cricket played in the West Indies was between local, often predominantly white, sides and English tourists – the Middlesex player Robert Slade Lucas toured the West Indies with a team in 1894–95, and two years later Arthur Priestley took a team to Barbados, Trinidad, and Jamaica, which included, for the first time, a match against a side styled "All West Indies", which the West Indians won. Lord Hawke's English team, including several English Test players, toured around the same time, playing Trinidad, Barbados and British Guiana (now Guyana).

Then in 1900 the white Trinidadian Aucher Warner, the brother of future England captain Pelham Warner, led a touring side to England, but none of the matches on this tour were given first-class status. Two winters later, in 1901–02, the Hampshire wicketkeeper Richard Bennett's XI went to the West Indies, and played three games against teams styled as the "West Indies", which the hosts won 2–1. In 1904–05, Lord Brackley's XI toured the Caribbean – winning both its games against "West Indies".

The tours to England continued in 1906 when Harold Austin led a West Indian side to England. His side played a number of county teams, and drew their game against an "England XI". However, that England XI only included one contemporary Test player – wicketkeeper Dick Lilley – and he had not been on England's most recent tour, their 1905–6 tour of South Africa. The Marylebone Cricket Club, which had taken over responsibility for arranging all official overseas England tours, visited the West Indies in 1910–11, and 1912–13 but after that there was no international cricket of any note until the West Indian team went to England in 1923. This tour did not include a game against an England team, but there was an end-of-season game against HDG Leveson-Gower's XI against a virtual England Test side at the Scarborough cricket festival, a traditional end-of-season game against a touring side at the English seaside resort of Scarborough, which Leveson-Gower's XI won by only four wickets. 1925–26 saw another MCC tour of the West Indies.

The MCC was eager to promote cricket throughout the British Empire, and on 31 May 1926 the West Indian Cricket Board, along with their New Zealand and Indian counterparts, was elected to the Imperial Cricket Conference (ICC), which previously consisted of the MCC and representatives of Australia and South Africa. Election to full membership of the ICC meant the West Indies could play official Test matches, which is the designation given to the most important international games, and the Windies became the fourth team actually to play a recognised Test match on 23 June 1928 when they took on England at Lord's in London. They did not, however, enjoy immediate success – the West Indies lost all three 3-day Tests in that 1928 tour by a long way, failing to score 250 runs in any of their six innings in that series. They also failed to dismiss England for under 350 runs in a series completely dominated by England.

· **The early Tests (1930s and 1940s)**

The West Indies team that toured Australia in 1930–31. The West Indies played 19 Tests in the 1930s in four series against England and one against Australia. The first four of these were played against an England team led by the Honourable Freddie Calthorpe that toured in 1929–30.

However, as Harold Gilligan was leading another English team to New Zealand at exactly the same time, this was not a full-strength England side. The series ended one-all, with the West Indies first ever Test victory being recorded on 26 February 1930. West Indian George Headley scored the most runs (703) in the rubber and Learie Constantine took the most wickets (18).

The West Indies toured Australia in 1930–31. They lost the Test series 4–1. The fifth and final Test showed some promise – batting first, the West Indies spent the first three days earning a 250-run lead with five wickets down in their second innings. A bold declaration was backed up by their bowlers, as Herman Griffith took four wickets and West Indies won by 30 runs to their first overseas Test victory. By the time the team left, they had left a good impression of themselves with the Australian public, although at first the team were faced with several cultural differences – for example, their hosts did not at first appreciate that the tourists' Roman Catholic beliefs would mean they would refuse to play golf on Sundays or engage in more ribald behaviour.

The West Indian sides of the time were always led by white men, and the touring party to Australia comprised seven whites and eleven "natives", and the West Indian Board of Control wrote to their Australian counterparts saying "that all should reside at the same hotels". Australia at the time had in place its "White Australia" policy, with the Australian Board having to guarantee to the Government that the non-whites would leave at the end of the tour. When the West Indians arrived in Sydney, the whites were immediately given a different hotel from the blacks. They complained, and thereafter their wishes were met. The tour lost a lot of money, part of which was due to the Great

Depression then affecting Australia. The West Indians won four and lost eight of their 14 first-class fixtures.

1933 saw another tour of England. Their hosts had just come back from defeating Australia in the infamous Bodyline series, where England's aggressive bowling at the body with a legside field attracted much criticism. England won the three-Test series of three-day Tests against the Windies 2–0. The second, drawn, Test at Old Trafford, Manchester, provided an intriguing footnote to the Bodyline controversy when Manny Martindale and Learie Constantine bowled Bodyline – fast, short-pitched balls aimed at the body – against the Englishmen, the only time they faced it in international cricket. The tactic did not work, as Douglas Jardine, the English captain who ordered his players to bowl it against the Australians, did not flinch as he scored his only Test century, making 127 out of England's 374.

· **Learie Constantine**

Another England tour of the West Indies followed in 1934–35. England won the first Test in Barbados on a poor pitch, affected by rain, and in a match where 309 runs were scored, England took a four-wicket victory. Both sides declared one of their innings closed to have their bowlers take advantage of the poor pitch. The second Test saw the Windies win by 217 runs, and a drawn third Test saw the series go to a decider at Sabina Park in Jamaica. A massive 270 not out from George Headley saw the Windies declare on 535 for 7. Despite a century from Les Ames, England could not avoid going down by an innings and 161 runs – the West Indies had secured their first Test series victory.

The West Indies toured England in 1939. England won the first Test at Lord's easily by 8 wickets, then there was a rain-affected draw in Manchester, and finally a high-scoring draw at the Oval in mid-August. The highlight of the series for the West Indies was George Headley scoring hundreds in both innings in the Lord's Test. With the clouds of World War II seemingly about to envelope Europe, the rest of the tour was cancelled and the Windies returned home. They would play no more Tests until 21 January 1948 saw the start of the first Test the West Indies played since the War, which resulted in a draw against the MCC side from England. The second Test was also drawn, with George Carew and Andy Ganteaume both making centuries. Ganteaume was then dropped, ending with a Test average of 112 – the highest in Test history. The West Indies won the final two Tests chasing sub-100 totals, and wrapped up the series 2–0, their first away-series victory.

In 1948, West Indies toured newly independent India for the first time for a five Test tour. The tour was preceded by a non-Test tour of Pakistan and followed by a similar short tour of Ceylon. After three high-scoring draws against the Indians, the West Indians wrapped up the fourth by an innings before a thrilling fifth Test, which left the Indians six runs away from victory with two wickets in hand as time ran out, so that the West Indies thus won the rubber 1–0. Carrying on from his hundred in the series against England, Everton Weekes set a record of scoring hundreds in five successive Test innings.

· **The post-War period (1950s)**

1950 saw another tour of England, the series saw the emergence for the West Indies of their great spinning duo,

Sonny Ramadhin and Alf Valentine. England won the first Test by 202 runs, but Valentine and Ramadhin's bowling would win the series for the visitors. The second Test saw the Windies put on 326 thanks to 106 from Allan Rae before Valentine (4 for 48) and Ramadhin (5 for 66) skittled England in the first innings. A mammoth 168 from Clyde Walcott saw England set a theoretical target of 601. Ramadhin's 6 for 86 and Valentine's 3 for 79 dismissed the hosts for 274. The spinning duo took 12 wickets, Frank Worrell made 261 and Everton Weekes 129 as the third Test went the Windies way by 10 wickets, the fourth saw 14 wickets from Valentine and Ramadhin and centuries from Rae and Worrell as England were defeated by an innings. The West Indies won the series 3–1.

In 1951–1952 the Windies visited Australia. The first Test saw a narrow defeat by three wickets, with the two spinners seemingly continuing their form with twelve wickets between them. The second Test was lost by seven wickets, as Australia replied to the Windies 362 and 290 with 567 (which included centuries from Lindsay Hassett and Keith Miller) and 137 for 2. 6 wickets from Worrell in the third Test saw Australia dismissed for only 82, and the Windies eventually won by six wickets to pull back to two-one down in the series. The fourth Test saw the series lost in a narrow defeat. Worrell, batting with an injured hand, scored 108 and helped the Windies to 272 before Australia made 216 in reply.

203 from the Windies left Australia a target of 260. 5 wickets from Valentine helped reduced the Aussies to 222 for 9, 38 short with 1 wicket remaining. It didn't happen, as some brilliant running between the wicket for Australia by Bill Johnston and Doug Ring saw West Indies lose their composure and the match. The fifth Test saw three batting

collapses, as Australia (116 and 377) beat Windies (78 and 213) by 202 runs to finish the rubber four-one winners. The West Indies then went on to New Zealand. In the first Test encounter between the two teams, the visitors scored a five wicket victory. In the second and final Test, Allan Rae scored 99, Jeffrey Stollmeyer 152, Frank Worrell 100 and Clyde Walcott 115 as the West Indies put on 546 for 6 declared. There wasn't enough time to bowl out the opposition twice though, as the hosts made 160 and were following-on at 17 for 1 when stumps were drawn, leaving the Windies series winners.

The Indians toured at the beginning of 1953. The Windies won the second of the five Tests that were played, with the others all being draws. The highlight of these games we Frank Worrell's 237 in the fifth Test, where all the three W's scored hundreds, as the West Indies scored a 1–0 series victory. Len Hutton led an MCC (England) side to the islands in 1953–1954. Sonny Ramadhin again starred for the Windies taking 23 wickets (no other West Indian took more than 8), as Walcott's 698 runs was more than 200 higher than second-placed West Indian, Everton Weekes. The five match rubber was drawn two-all.

Australia came and conquered in 1954–1955. After the Aussies made 515 in the first innings of the first Test, the Windies went down by 9 wickets. Then the Windies 382 was put in the shade by 600 for 9 declared by the visitors as the second Test was drawn. A low-scoring third Test saw Australia (257 and 133 for 2) beat the hosts (182 and 207) by 8 wickets. After Australia scored 668 in the fourth Test, the series was lost, although a double century from captain Denis Atkinson and a world-record stand for the seventh wicket allowed the Windies to reach 510 and draw the Test. The fifth Test saw the West Indies win the toss and bat.

Walcott's 155 was the highest score of their 357.

The Australians then batted and batted, in total for 245.4 overs in the 6-day Test, as they put on 758 for 8 declared, with five players making centuries. 319 in the West Indies' second innings left them defeated by an innings and 82 runs in the Test, and by three games to nil in the series. Walcott set records by scoring five hundreds, and hundreds in both innings of a match twice. A four-Test tour of New Zealand followed in February 1956. After two wins by an innings and one by 9 wickets, the Windies were surprised by the Kiwis in the fourth, dismissing them for 145 and 77 as they recorded their first ever Test win in their 45th Test.

John Goddard returned to captain the West Indians for a five-Test tour of England in 1957, which was lost three-nil, with England having the better of the two draws. Then 1957–1958 Gerry Alexander led a team that defeated Pakistan three-one. It was in this series in Jamaica that Garry Sobers scored 365 not out to record what was then the highest score in Test match cricket. Alexander went on to lead the West Indies to a three-nil win over five Tests in India, and a 2–1 defeat by Pakistan in a three match rubber in the following winter. In 1959–1960 he led as West Indies went down one-nil at home in a five-match series with England.

· A period of mixed fortunes (1960s)

Despite being a region where whites are a minority, until 1960 West Indies were always captained by white cricketers, though this was more social than racial discrimination. Throughout the 1950s, social theorist CLR James, the increasingly political former cricketer Learie Constantine and others called for a black captain. Constantine himself had stood in for Jackie Grant in the field against England on the 1934–35 tour, and George Headley captained the West Indies in the First Test against England in 1947–48 when the appointed, white captain, John Goddard was injured. However, no black was appointed as captain for a whole series until Frank Worrell was chosen to lead West Indies in their tour of Australia in 1960–61. In his three years as captain, Worrell moulded a bunch of talented but raw cricketers into probably the best team in the world.

In 1960, Australia were the best team in the world but on their way down, while West Indies were on their way up. It so happened that when they met,the two teams were of almost equal strength. The result was a series that has been recognised as one of the greatest of all time. The first Test in Brisbane was the first Test ever to end in a tie, which in cricket means the side batting last has been dismissed with scores level. The teams shared the next two Tests. In the fourth, Australia's last pair of Ken Mackay and Lindsay Kline played out the last 100 minutes of the match to earn a draw, while Australia won the final Test and the series by two wickets. One of the days of play was attended by a world-record crowd of 90,800. Such was the impression created by Worrell's team that the newly instituted trophy for the series between the two teams was named the Frank Worrell Trophy.

West Indies beat India 5–0 at home next year, and in 1963, they beat a fine English team by three matches to one. The Lord's Test of this series saw a famous finish. With two balls left, England needed six runs to win, and West Indies one wicket. The non-striker was Colin Cowdrey, who had his left arm in a sling, having fractured it earlier in the day. However, David Allen safely played out the last two balls and the match ended in a draw. Worrell retired at the end of the series. The selectors picked Garry Sobers to succeed him.

Worrell did, however, serve as the team manager when West Indies hosted Australia in 1964–65. The matches against Australia were bitterly fought, with accusations about Charlie Griffith's action and bouncer wars. The West Indies won this series 2–1 to be the unofficial world champions. Sobers was not as good at man-management as Worrell and cracks soon began to appear. Often it was his individual brilliance that made the difference between a win and a loss. Throughout the 1960s, West Indies bowling was led by Wes Hall, Griffith, Lance Gibbs and Sobers himself. Hall and Griffith faded and then retired by the end of the decade, but WI could find no replacement for them till the mid-1970s.

Sobers was at his best in England in 1966, scoring 722 runs and taking 20 wickets in the five Tests. Three times he topped 150, and the 163* at Lord's turned a certain defeat into a near victory. West Indies won 3–1. England toured the West Indies in 1967–68 for a series that became noted for England's deliberate slow play. West Indies were forced to follow on in the first Test but saved it without difficulty. The second Test was played on an underprepared wicket at Kingston. England won an important toss and scored 376. The bounce of the wicket having become very uneven, West Indies collapsed to 143 and followed on. On the fourth day in the second innings, a disputed decision led to a crowd riot, and the match had to be stopped for some time.

In a curious decision, the West Indian Cricket Board (WICB) agreed to add a 75-minute sixth day to compensate for the lost time. Sobers played an outstanding innings of 113 not out, which allowed West Indies to set England a target of 159 in 155 minutes. England just about saved the game, losing eight wickets for 68. In the fourth Test West Indies gained a first innings lead of 122 at Port-of-Spain, but with the second innings score at 92 for 2, Sobers, frustrated by England's slow over rates and wanting to give himself a chance, albeit a small one, to win, surprisingly declared the innings, a decision for which he was widely criticised at the time. England were set a target of 215 in 165 minutes and they achieved it with 3 minutes to spare. West Indies made one last effort to win the final Test, but England drew it with only wicket left in their second innings. West Indies lost the series 0–1, the first defeat since 1960–61.

Australia and Bill Lawry had their revenge in 1968–69, when West Indies lost the away series 1–3. New Zealand managed to draw the series that followed, and then in 1969 West Indies were defeated 0–2 in England.

· **World dominance (1970s)**

West Indies' woes overflowed into the 1970s. At home in 1970–71, they lost to India for the first time. In the next year, a five Test series against New Zealand cricket team ended with no team coming close to winning one. A major find in the New Zealand series was Lawrence Rowe, who started off with a double century and century on his debut. Under Rohan Kanhai's captaincy, West Indies showed the first signs of revival. Australia won the closely fought 1972–73 series in the Caribbean by two Tests. With Sobers back – but Kanhai still the captain – West Indies defeated England 2–0 in 1973. This included a win by an innings and 226 runs at Lord's, their biggest win against England. The return series in West Indies ended 1–1, though the home team was the better side. Rowe continued his run scoring three centuries including a 302 at Kingston. The final Test of this 1973–74 series marked the end of an era in West Indies cricket – it was the last Test of both Garry Sobers and Rohan Kanhai, and marked the emergence of fast bowler Andy Roberts.

The new captain Clive Lloyd had made his first appearance in Test cricket in 1966 and had since become a fixture in the side. His avuncular, bespectacled appearance and a stoop near the shoulders masked the fact that he was a very fine fielder, especially in the covers, and a devastating stroke player. Lloyd's first assignment was the tour of India in 1974–75. West Indies won the first two Tests comfortably. Gordon Greenidge started his career with 107 and 93 in the first Test. Vivian Richards failed on his debut, but scored 192* in his second. India fought back to win the next two, but Lloyd hit 242* in the final Test to win the series.

· **Flag of the West Indies cricket team prior to 1999**

West Indies won the inaugural World Cup in England in 1975, defeating Australia in the final. Then in 1975–76 they toured Australia, only to lose 1–5 in the six-Test series, and then beat India at home two-one in a four Test series later that same winter. It was in Australia that the quick bowler Michael Holding made his first appearance. Colin Croft and Joel Garner made their debuts the next year, and Malcolm Marshall two years after. In the span of about four years, West Indies brought together a bowling line-up of a quality that had rarely been seen before. The tour of India had seen the debut of Vivian Richards, arguably the finest West Indian batsman ever, and Gordon Greenidge, who joined a strong batting line-up that already included Alvin Kallicharran and opener Roy Fredericks in addition to Rowe and Lloyd. These players formed the nucleus of the side that became recognised as world Test match champions until the beginning of the 1990s.

Next came a tour of England in 1976. In a TV interview before the series, English captain Tony Greig commented that the West Indies tend to do badly under pressure and that "we'll make them grovel". This comment, especially as it came from a South African-born player, touched a raw nerve of the West Indians. Throughout the series, the English batsmen were subjected to what was described by the English press as very hostile bowling, but was rather reflective of a solid pace attack, and what the Windies had faced in Australia before. After the first two Tests ended in draws, West Indies won the next three. Of the many heroes for West Indies, Richards stood out with 829 runs in four Tests. He hit 232 at Trent Bridge and 291 at the Oval. Greenidge scored three hundreds, two of which were on the difficult wicket at Old Trafford. Roberts and Holding shared 55 wickets between them, Holding's 8 for 92 and 6 for 57 on the unhelpful wicket at the Oval being a superlative effort.

West Indies won a home series against a tough Pakistan side in 1976–77. A few months later, the World Series Cricket (WSC) controversy broke out. Most of the West Indian players signed up with Kerry Packer, an Australian TV magnate who was attempting to set up his own international cricket competition. The Australian team that toured West Indies the next year included no Packer players. West Indies Cricket Board fielded a full-strength team under the argument that none of the West Indies players had refused to play, but disputes arose in the matter of payment and about the selection of certain players. Before the third Test, Lloyd resigned his captaincy. Within two days all the other WSC-contracted players also withdrew. Alvin Kallicharran captained the team for the remaining Tests of the series, which the Windies won 3–1.

WICB allowed the WSC players to appear in the 1979 World Cup, and the West Indies retained the title with little difficulty. By the end of 1979, the WSC disputes were resolved. Kallicharran was deposed after losing a six-match series one-nil in India and Lloyd returned as captain for a tour against a full-strength Australia (where the Windies won two-nil, with one draw) and New Zealand. The latter tour was full of controversy.

New Zealand won the first Test at Dunedin by one wicket, but West Indies were never happy with the umpiring. West Indian discontent boiled over the next Test at Christchurch. While running into bowl, Colin Croft deliberately shouldered the umpire Fred Goodall. When Goodall went to talk to Lloyd about Croft's behaviour, he had to walk all the way to meet the West Indian captain, as the latter did not move an inch from his position at the slips. After tea on the third day, West Indies refused to take the field unless Goodall was removed. They were persuaded to continue, and it took intense negotiations between the two boards to keep the tour on track. The Kiwis won the three match series after the second and third Tests ended in draws. Nevertheless, the defeat proved to be the West Indies last Test series loss for the next 15 years.

After losing their first series of the 1980s in March 1980, the West Indies went throughout the rest of the decade undefeated.

The 1980s started with a one-nil victory away to England over five Tests, one-nil away to Pakistan over four Tests, two-nil home to England over four Tests and a one-all draw away to Australia. Then in 1982–83, a West Indian rebel team toured apartheid South Africa. It was led by Lawrence Rowe and included prominent players like Alvin

Kallicharran, Colin Croft, Collis King and Sylvester Clarke. WICB banned the players for life (which was later revoked), and some were refused entry back home. However, the rebels managed another tour the next year, which included most of the players of the original team.

Despite this loss of talent, the official Windies side continued to dominate. During this time, the West Indies established themselves as one of Test cricket's all-time great sides, peaking perhaps on their tour of England in 1984, where they won the series 5–0, the only time in Test cricket history the touring side has whitewashed a five-test series. This was followed by a second "blackwash" against England at home in 1985–86. At the same time, the West Indies established the then-record of 11 consecutive Test victories, which was part of a still-standing record of 27 Tests without defeat. In the period from 1980 to 1985–86 they won 10 out of 11 Test series, the 1981–82 series in Australia being drawn 1–1. The West Indies' only notable defeat in this period was in the one-day arena, when, to general surprise, they lost to India in the final of the 1983 World Cup.

West Indian captain Lloyd retired from Test cricket at the end of the 1984–85 series against Australia. In total Lloyd had captained West Indies in 74 Test matches, winning 36 of them. Vivian Richards was Lloyd's successor, and continued the run of success. Meanwhile, a change of old guard was also happening. Joel Garner and Michael Holding had retired by 1987. A major find was Curtly Ambrose, who was as tall as Garner and equally effective with the ball.

Courtney Walsh, who made his first appearance in 1984, bowled with an action that resembled Holding. Ian Bishop also had a similar action, and was as good a bowler till injuries interrupted his career. Patrick Patterson was faster than all the rest, but had a short career. Marshall still was the finest fast bowler in the world. But the batting was beginning to show signs of weakness, despite the presence of Richards, Greenidge and Desmond Haynes. West Indies failed to qualify for the semifinals of the 1987 World Cup. By the end of the 1980s, while still good were very beatable, they had lost the aura of invincibility that they had till the middle of the decade. Finding good replacements for senior players was again becoming a problem.

· Fall from grace (1990s–2000s)

During the early 1990s, the West Indies team was dealt a great blow with the retirement of its star players like Richards, Greenidge, Dujon and Marshall (who all retired after the away series against England in 1991), bringing an end of an era of strength. This left a youthful and inexperienced side. After Richards' retirement the only players with significant experience were Richie Richardson (who was appointed the new captain of the side), Desmond Haynes (who was soon dropped), Gus Logie (who was recalled), Courtney Walsh (who was now the leader of the West Indian pace attack) and Roger Harper (who came and went).

However, this did not immediately affect their performance. Richie Richardson proved to be a decent successor to Richards. A new crop of young players emerged such as Brian Lara, Curtly Ambrose, Ian Bishop, Jimmy Adams, Carl Hooper, Phil Simmons, Keith Arthurton and Winston Benjamin. It was five more years before the West Indies lost a series, but they had a number of close shaves before then. Making a comeback to international cricket, South Africa played its first Test match in

Bridgetown, a match which was attended by fewer than 10,000 people because of a boycott. Needing 201 to win on the last day, South Africa reached 123 for 2 before Ambrose and Walsh took the remaining 8 wickets for 25 runs. In 1992–93, the West Indies defeated Australia by one run in Adelaide, where a loss would have cost them the series. In 1994–95, the West Indies salvaged a draw in India when, after losing the first Test and drawing the second, they secured a win in the third. In 1992, the West Indies once again failed to qualify for the World Cup semi-finals.

Australia finally defeated the West Indies 2–1 in 1994–95 to become the unofficial world champions of Test cricket. The 1996 World Cup ended with a defeat in the semi-final, which forced Richie Richardson to end his career. The captaincy passed over to Courtney Walsh and then in 1998 to Brian Lara. The West Indies made their first ever official tour to South Africa in 1998–99. It was a disaster, starting with player revolts and ending with a 5–0 defeat. The 1999 World Cup campaign ended in the group stages. The next year, England won a series against the West Indies for the first time in thirty-one years. The West Indies ended the decade with another 5–0 defeat, this time in Australia.

For most of the 1990s, the West Indian batting lineup was dominated by Brian Lara. Lara became a regular in the side after the retirement of Viv Richards in 1991. In 1993–94, he scored 375 against England in Antigua, breaking Sobers' world record for the highest individual score in Test cricket. He continued his fine form playing for Warwickshire in the 1994 English County Championship, posting seven first-class hundreds in eight innings (including the Test match 375). The last of these was 501 not out against Durham, which improved upon Hanif Mohammad's thirty-five-year-old record as the highest score in first-class cricket. The

West Indian bowling attack was spearheaded by Curtly Ambrose and Courtney Walsh, the latter setting a then world record of 519 wickets. However, these two had both retired by 2001, and their successors failed to maintain the high standards that Ambrose and Walsh had set. Despite the emergence of some good batsmen like Shivnarine Chanderpaul and Ramnaresh Sarwan, Brian Lara remained the crucial figure of the side.

After a 2–0 defeat by New Zealand in 1999–00, Lara was replaced as captain by Jimmy Adams, who initially enjoyed series wins against Zimbabwe and Pakistan. However, a 3–1 defeat by England and a 5–0 whitewash by Australia saw him replaced by Carl Hooper for the 2000–01 visit by South Africa. By the time Lara was restored to the captaincy in 2002–03, series had been lost to South Africa, Sri Lanka, Pakistan, New Zealand and India. The only series win of note was against India (although Zimbabwe and Bangladesh were also beaten) as the West Indies plummeted to eighth place in the world-rankings, below all the other established Test nations.

After losing the first series of his second captaincy period to world champions Australia, Lara secured success against Sri Lanka and Zimbabwe, before another poor run saw 3–0 defeats in 4-Test series against both South Africa and England. In the drawn fourth Test against England, Lara became the only man to regain the world record for highest individual Test score by scoring 400 not out, once again in Antigua, bettering Matthew Hayden's 380 against Zimbabwe the previous year. The West Indies were then whitewashed 4–0 in England. Lara's last act as captain was to win the 2004 ICC Champions Trophy, a one-day competition second only to the Cricket World Cup, at the Oval, London – a win that was a welcome surprise for the

Caribbean which had just been hit by Hurricane Ivan.

- **Player, Board disputes**

This joy was short-lived as a major dispute broke out in 2005 between the West Indian Players Association (WIPA) and the Cricket Board. The point of contention was clause 5 of the tour contract which gave WICB the sole and exclusive right to arrange for sponsorship, advertising, licensing, merchandising and promotional activities relating to WICB or any WICB Team. Digicel were the sponsors of the West Indian Team, while most of the players had contracts with Cable & Wireless.

This conflict, coupled with a payment dispute meant that the West Indies initially announced a team absent Lara and a number of other leading West Indians for South Africa's visit in 2004–05, leading to Shivnarine Chanderpaul becoming captain. Some of these players did, in the end, compete. However, the dispute had not been resolved and rumbled on, leading to a second-string side being named for the tour of Sri Lanka in 2005. A resolution did not arise until October 2005, when a full-strength side was finally named for the 2005–06 tour of Australia. It was on this tour that Brian Lara overtook Australian Allan Border as the highest run-scorer in Test match cricket, despite the West Indies losing the series 3–0.

In 2009, another dispute erupted when many senior players decided not to take part over pay and contract issues. The WICB chose a second-string side to take part in a series against Bangladesh and the Champions Trophy. In 2012, ICC decided to get involved in order to resolve this long standing dispute.

In 2014, another dispute between WICB and West Indian Players Association (WIPA) led to the team's Indian tour being curtailed. The bone of contention was a protracted payment structure.

In 2015, Players has made themselves unavailable for tests, and with Jason Holder being thrust into the role of captaincy, and was met with much distrust between veteran bowlers and Holder and the administration and selectors. As a result, West Indies lost 21 matches by an innings since 1995–2015, when the team never lost more than 4 matches by over an innings combined from 1966 to 1995.

· **Rebuilding and T20 success (2010s)**

When Twenty20 cricket began to be contested full force beginning with the 2007 World Twenty20 in South Africa, the West Indies began to develop and realize an advantage of possessing and developing Richards-style batsmen who could devastate bowling attacks with power. As well, many West Indian batsmen put an emphasis on power to prepare for Twenty20 play as it offered them their most lucrative contracts. Foremost among the hard hitters was Chris Gayle, who both hit the first T20 international century and became the first to hit two.

At the 2012 World Twenty20 in Sri Lanka, the West Indies beat Australia in the semifinals and then beat the hosts by 32 runs to win their third ICC world championship and their first since Richards, Holding. and Lloyd had won the 1979 World Cup. In the 2016 World Twenty20, they beat host India in the semifinals after a successful chase and were still cheered back at their hotel by local and traveling fans as they advanced to face England in the final, which they won by four wickets after Carlos Brathwaite hit four consecutive sixes off Ben Stokes with 19 runs required off the final over. In contrast to being 8th in the ICC Test Rankings and 9th in the ICC ODI Rankings, the West Indies entered the match as second in the ICC T20 rankings behind India.

- **West Indies cricket team**

The West Indies cricket team, nicknamed the Windies, is a multi-national men's cricket team representing the mainly English-speaking countries and territories in the Caribbean region and administered by Cricket West Indies. The players on this composite team are selected from a chain of fifteen Caribbean nation-states and territories. As of 26 November 2022, the West Indies cricket team is ranked eighth in Tests, and tenth in ODIs and seventh in T20Is in the official ICC rankings.

From the mid-late 1970s to the early 1990s, the West Indies team was the strongest in the world in both Test and One Day International cricket. A number of cricketers who were considered among the best in the world have hailed from the West Indies: Garfield Sobers, Lance Gibbs, George Headley, Brian Lara, Vivian Richards, Clive Lloyd, Malcolm Marshall, Alvin Kallicharran, Andy Roberts, Rohan Kanhai, Frank Worrell, Clyde Walcott, Everton Weekes, Curtly Ambrose, Michael Holding, Courtney Walsh, Joel Garner, and Wes Hall have all been inducted into the ICC Cricket Hall of Fame.

The West Indies have won the ICC Cricket World Cup twice (1975 and 1979, when it was styled the Prudential Cup), the ICC T20 World Cup twice (2012 and 2016, when it was styled World Twenty20), the ICC Champions Trophy once

(2004), the ICC Under 19 Cricket World Cup once (2016), and have also finished as runners-up in the Cricket World Cup (1983), the Under 19 Cricket World Cup (2004), and the ICC Champions Trophy (2006). The West Indies appeared in three consecutive World Cup finals (1975, 1979 and 1983), and were the first team to win back-to-back World Cups (1975 and 1979), both of these records have been surpassed only by Australia, who appeared in 4 consecutive World Cup Finals (1996, 1999, 2003 and 2007) winning 3 consecutive World Cups (1999, 2003 and 2007).

- **History of the West Indian cricket team**

Learie Constantine, who played Test cricket in the 1920s and 1930s, was one of the first great West Indian players.Darren Sammy. The West Indies have won three major tournament titles: the Champions Trophy once, and the World Twenty20 twice. Both World T20s were won with Sammy as captain, making him the only West Indian captain besides Clive Lloyd with multiple ICC tournament victories.

The history of the West Indies cricket team began in the 1890s, when the first representative sides were selected to play visiting English sides. The WICB joined the sport's international ruling body, the Imperial Cricket Conference, in 1926, and played their first official international match, granted Test status, in 1928, thus becoming the fourth Test 'nation'. In their early days in the 1930s, the side represented the British colonies that would later form the West Indies Federation plus British Guiana.

The last series the West Indies played before the outbreak of the Second World War was against England in 1939. There followed a hiatus that lasted until January 1948 when the MCC toured the West Indies. Of the West Indies players in that first match after the war only Gerry Gomez, George Headley, Jeffrey Stollmeyer, and Foffie Williams had previously played Test cricket. In 1948, leg spinner Wilfred Ferguson became the first West Indian bowler to take ten wickets in a Test, finishing with 11/229 in a match against England; later that same year Hines Johnson became the first West Indies fast bowler to achieve the feat, managing 10/96 against the same opponents.

The West Indies defeated England for the first time at Lord's on 29 June 1950. Ramadhin and Alf Valentine were the architects of the victory which inspired a calypso by Lord Beginner. Later on 16 August 1950, completed a 3–1 series win when they won at The Oval. Although blessed with some great players in their early days as a Test team, their successes remained sporadic until the 1960s when the side changed from a white-dominated to a black-dominated side under the successive captaincies of Frank Worrell and Gary Sobers.

By the late 1970s, the West Indies led by Clive Lloyd had a side recognised as unofficial world champions, a reputation they retained throughout the 1980s. During these glory years, the West Indies were noted for their four-man fast bowling attack, backed up by some of the best batsmen in the world. In 1976, fast bowler Michael Holding took 14/149 in the OvalTest against England, setting a record which still stands for best bowling figures in a Test by a West Indies bowler. The 1980s saw the team set a then-record streak of 11 consecutive Test victories in 1984 and inflict two 5–0 "blackwashes" on England.

Throughout the 1990s and 2000s, however, West Indian cricket declined, largely owing to the failure of the West Indian Cricket Board to move the game from an amateur pastime to a professional sport, coupled with the general economic decline in West Indian countries, and the team struggling to retain its past glory. Victory in the 2004 Champions Trophy and a runner-up showing in the 2006 Champions Trophy left some hopeful, but it was not until the inception of Twenty20 cricket that the West Indies began to regain a place among the cricketing elite and among cricket fans, as they developed ranks of players capable of taking over games with their power hitting, including Chris Gayle, Kieron Pollard, Marlon Samuels, Lendl Simmons, DJ Bravo, Andre Russell and Carlos Brathwaite.

They beat Australia and then host Sri Lanka in the 2012 World Twenty20 to win their first ICC world championship since the 1979 World Cup and then bested England to win the 2016 World Twenty20, making them the first team to win the World Twenty20 twice. As an added bonus, the West Indies also became the first to win both the men's and women's World Twenty20 on the same day, as the women's team beat three-time defending champion Australia for their first ICC world title immediately beforehand.

· **Flag and anthem**

Former flag of the West Indies cricket team used until 1999. This flag became public domain but the current version is copyrighted.Most cricketing nations use their own national flags for cricketing purposes. However, as the West Indies represent a number of independent states and dependencies, there is no natural choice of flag. The WICB has, therefore, developed an insignia showing a palm tree and cricket stumps on a small sunny island.

The insignia, on a maroon background, makes up the West Indian flag. The background sometimes has a white stripe above a green stripe, which is separated by a maroon stripe, passing horizontally through the middle of the background. Prior to 1999, the WICB(C) had used a similar insignia featuring a cabbage palm tree and an island, but there were no stumps and, instead of the sun, there was the constellation Orion. It was designed in 1923 by Sir Algernon Aspinall, then Secretary of the West India Committee. Around the same time in the 1920s the suggested motto for the West Indies team was "Nec curat Orion leones", which comes from a quote by Horace, meaning that Orion, as symbolical of the West Indies XI, does not worry about the lions.For ICC tournaments, "Rally 'Round the West Indies" by David Rudder is used as the team's anthem.

· List of cricket grounds in the West Indies

The following eleven stadiums have been used for at least one Test match. The number of Tests played at each venue followed by the number of One Day Internationals and twenty20 internationals played at that venue is in brackets as of 2 April 2021.

Queen's Park Oval – Port of Spain, Trinidad (61/73/6): The Queen's Park Oval has hosted more Test matches than any other ground in the Caribbean and first hosted a Test match in 1930. The ground is considered one of the most picturesque venues in the world of cricket, featuring the view Trinidad's Northern Range. It has a capacity of over 18,000.

Kensington Oval – Bridgetown, Barbados (55/44/23):Kensington Oval hosted the region's first Test match in 1930 and is recognised as the 'Mecca' of West Indies cricket.

Its capacity was increased from 15,000 to 28,000 for the 2007 World Cup and down to its current capacity of 11,000 post – World Cup. It has hosted two ICC world finals – the 2007 Cricket World Cup Final, which Australia won over Sri Lanka, and the 2010 World Twenty20 Final, which England won against Australia.

Bourda – Georgetown, Guyana (30/11/0): Bourda first hosted a Test match in 1930. It was the only Test ground in South America (until the use of Providence), and the only one below sea level and with its own moat (to prevent the pitch from frequent flooding). It has a capacity of around 22,000. It is remembered for the Pitch Invasion during an April 1999, One Day International between Australia and the West Indies, with Australia needing 3 runs to tie and 4 to win off the last ball, a full scale pitch invasion, resulted in the match being deemed a tie, due to the stumps having been stolen before the West Indian team could effect a run out.

Sabina Park – Kingston, Jamaica (54/41/6): Sabina Park first hosted a Test match in 1930. The Blue Mountains, which are famed for their coffee, form the backdrop. Sabina Park played host to Garry Sobers' then world-record 365 not out. In 1998, the Test against England was abandoned here on the opening day because the pitch was too dangerous. It has a capacity of 15,000.

Antigua Recreation Ground – St John's, Antigua (22/11/0): Antigua Recreation Ground first hosted a Test in 1981. Three Test triple centuries have been scored on this ground: Chris Gayle's 317 in 2005, and Brian Lara's world record scores of 375 in 1994 and 400 not out in 2004. The historic stadium was removed from the roster of grounds hosting international matches in June 2006, to make way for the island's new cricket stadium, being constructed 3 miles outside the capital city expected to be completed in time for its hosting of matches for Cricket World Cup 2007. However, after the abandoned Test match between England and the West Indies in February 2009 at the new North Sound ground, Test cricket returned to the ARG.

Darren Sammy National Cricket Stadium – Gros Islet, St Lucia (10/26/17): Originally the Beauséjour Cricket Ground, first hosted a Test in 2003. It has a capacity of 12,000. This was the first stadium in the Caribbean to host a day-night cricket match. The match was between the West Indies and Zimbabwe. New Zealand was scheduled to play a test in 2014 to mark the return to Test cricket after a break of 8 years. Following the West Indies' victory in the 2016 World Twenty20, the St. Lucian government renamed the venue after captain Sammy, a native St. Lucian, with another St. Lucian – Johnson Charles – having a stand named in his honor after also being part of the 2012 and 2016 championship squads.

Warner Park Stadium – Basseterre, St Kitts (3/18/10): The Warner Park Sporting Complex hosted its first One Day International on 23 May 2006 and its first Test match on 22 June 2006. The stadium has a permanent capacity of 8,000, with provisions for temporary stands to enable the hosting figure to past 10,000.

Providence Stadium – Georgetown, Guyana (2/24/8): The Providence Stadium hosted its first One Day International on 28 March 2007 for the 2007 Cricket World Cup and its first Test match on 22 March 2008. The stadium has a permanent capacity of 15,000, and is to host Test cricket instead of Bourda.

Sir Vivian Richards Stadium – North Sound, Antigua (12/20/4): The Sir Viv Richards Stadium hosted its first One Day International on 27 March 2007 for the 2007 Cricket World

Cup and its first Test match on 30 May 2008. The stadium has a permanent capacity of 10,000, and is to host Test cricket instead of the Antigua Recreation Ground.

Windsor Park Stadium – Roseau, Dominica (5/4/4): Windsor Park is another home venue for the West Indian team. Construction first started on it in 2005, and it finally opened in October 2007, too late to serve as a venue for the 2007 Cricket World Cup. It hosts first-class cricket and hosted its first test on 6 July 2011 against India, however it held its first One Day International on 26 July 2009. It has a seating capacity of 12,000.

Three further stadia have been used for One Day Internationals, or Twenty20 Internationals but not Test matches. The number of One Day Internationals and Twenty20 Internationals played at each venue is shown in the table below:

· **Clothing**

Viv Richards, who has a Test batting average of 50.23 from 121 matches, captained the West Indies from 1985–86 to 1991, a period throughout which the West Indies were the best Test match side in the world.When playing one-day cricket, the Windies wear a maroon-coloured shirt and trousers. The shirt also sports the logo of the West Indian Cricket Board and the name of their suppliers Castore on the sleeves of their jerseys. The one-day cap is maroon with the WICB logo on the left of the front, with two yellow stripes.

When playing first-class cricket, in addition to their cricket flannels West Indian fielders sometimes wear a maroon sunhat with a wide brim or a maroon baggy cap. The WICB logo is on the front of the hat. Helmets are coloured similarly. The sweater was edged with Maroon, green and grey. Gold was added to the stripes in the early 2000s. The design reverted to a simple maroon facing when the West Indies began wearing fleeces. In 2020 they again wore the traditional cable knit sweaters edged with Maroon and Green. When the team toured they wore maroon caps but in test matches in the Caribbean, it was customary for the team to wear dark blue caps until the late 1970s. The blazers awarded for home tests were dark blue with white and green facings. An example is displayed in the museum at Lord's. After c 1977 home and away teams both wore maroon caps and the blazers were the same colours.

During World Series Cricket, coloured uniforms were adopted. The initial West Indies uniform was pink and was later changed to maroon to match their Test match caps. Grey was also added as a secondary colour. In some of their uniforms grey has been dominant over the traditional maroon. Some uniforms had green, yellow or white as accent colour.

Former uniform suppliers were and BLK (2017-2019), Joma (2015-2017) Woodworm (2008-2015), Admiral (2000-2005), Asics (1999 World Cup), UK Sportsgear (1997-1998), ISC (1992-1996) and Adidas (1979-1991).

· **West Indies women's cricket team**

The West Indies women's cricket team enjoy a much lower profile than the men's team. They played 11 Test matches between 1975–76 and 1979, winning once, losing three times, and drawing the other games. Since then, they have only played one further Test match, a draw game against Pakistan in 2003–04.

They also have an infrequent record in One Day Internationals. A team from Trinidad and Tobago and a team from Jamaica played in the first women's World Cup in 1973, with both sides faring poorly, finishing fifth and sixth respectively out of a field of seven. The Windies united as a team to play their first ODI in 1979, but thereafter did not play until the 1993 World Cup. The side has never been one of the leading sides in the world, however, since the 2013 World Cup, where the team finished runner-ups, the team has improved reasonably well. Their main success being achieving second place in the International Women's Cricket Council Trophy, a competition for the second tier of women's national cricket teams, in 2003. Their overall record in one-dayers is to have played 177, won 80, lost 91 with one tie and 5 no results .

Because of the women's side's relatively low profile, there are few well-known names in the game. The most notable is probably Nadine George, a wicket-keeper/batsman, who became the first, and to date only, West Indian woman to score a Test century, in Karachi, Pakistan in 2003–04. George is a prominent supporter of sport in the West Indies, and in particular, in her native St Lucia, and in 2005 was made an MBE by the Prince of Wales for services to sport.

2016 saw the West Indies women win their first ICC world championship – the 2016 Women's World Twenty20, after beating three-time defending champion Australia by eight wickets at Eden Gardens with members of the men's team in the crowd to support.

www.ingramcontent.com/pod-product-compliance
Lightning Source LLC
Chambersburg PA
CBHW061642130726
47996CB00003B/1413